Maths Activity Book

for ages 4-5

This CGP book is bursting with bright and colourful Maths activities for children in Reception.

It's a brilliant way to introduce the essential topics — and it's stacks of fun too!

Helpful Hints

- A grown-up can help you read the questions. Let them know what you've been learning at school.

- Find a nice place to work. Make sure you're comfortable at your desk or table.

- Use a pencil to write or draw your answers. You can use coloured pencils to colour in the pictures.

- Work neatly, and try to keep your pencil inside the lines.

- Writing the numbers nice and clearly is really important — you can practise this on a separate piece of paper.

- The 'Turkey Trouble' activity in the centre uses maths skills from the whole book — you may want to save this until last.

Published by CGP

ISBN: 978 1 78908 603 4

Editors: Michael Bushell, Ben Train

With thanks to Ruth Greenhalgh, Joanne Haslett and Gail Renaud for the proofreading.
With thanks to Jan Greenway for the copyright research.

Printed and bound by Bell and Bain Ltd, Glasgow.
Cover and graphics used throughout the book © www.edu-clips.com
Cover design concept by emc design ltd.

Text, design, layout and original illustrations
© Coordination Group Publications Ltd. (CGP) 2020
All rights reserved.

Photocopying this book is not permitted, even if you have a CLA licence.
Extra copies are available from CGP with next day delivery • 0800 1712 712 • www.cgpbooks.co.uk

Contents

The Numbers 1-10	2
Adding	4
Taking Away	6
The Numbers 11-20	8
More Adding	10
More Taking Away	12
Puzzle: Turkey Trouble	14
Odd and Even Numbers	16
Ordering	18
Doubling	20
Halving	22
2D Shapes	24
3D Shapes	26
Patterns	28
Colour by Numbers	30

The Numbers 1-10

How It Works

Count the coins.

1   2   3   4   5

6   7   8   9   10

There are 10 coins.

Now Try These

Join the dots to write the numbers.

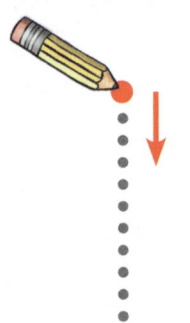  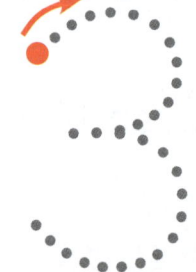 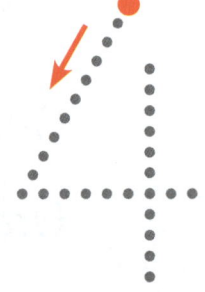

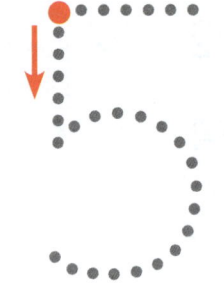   

 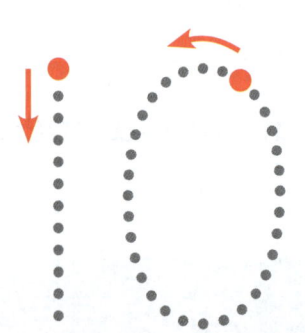

How many hats are there? Colour them in.

☐ hats

Draw a circle round the group that is the odd one out.

Count the crabs hiding below.

☐ crabs

You know your numbers! Give the box a big tick.

Adding

How It Works

Count the frogs. Then add them together.

 and  makes

2 and **3** makes **5**

Now Try These

Add the birds together. Colour in the total.

  and  makes

☐ and ☐ makes ☐

Suzy is counting grasshoppers.

  add  is

Add the grasshoppers. Circle the number.

 1   2   3   4   5   6   7   8   9

Count the acorns to fill in the boxes.

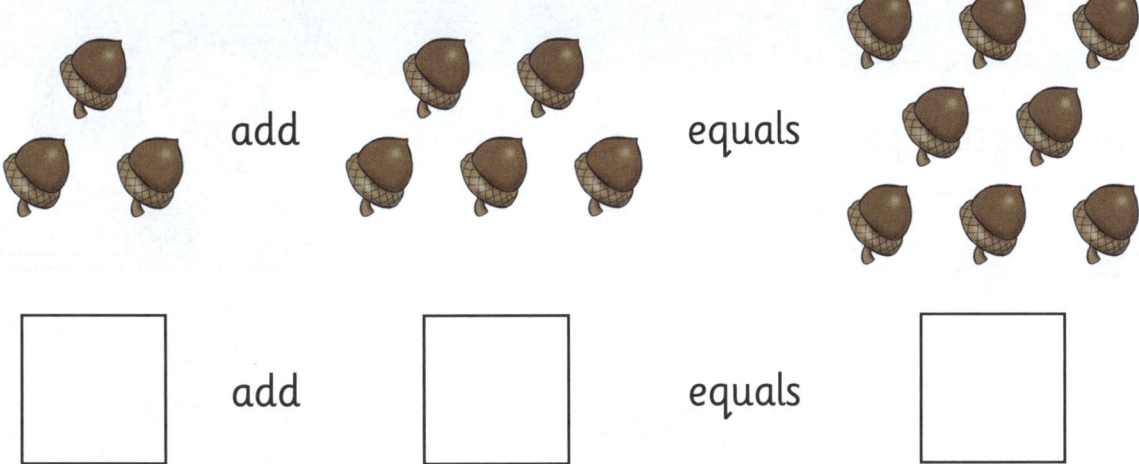

☐ add ☐ equals ☐

Circle 4 eggs (🥚) and 4 feathers (🪶) hiding in the forest.

Now add them together.   4 add 4 equals ☐

Your adding up skills are amazing! Tick the box. ☐

Taking Away

How It Works

Count 4 jigsaw pieces.

Take 1 away.

    →

4 take away 1 is 3.

Now Try These

Ali has five bricks. She gives 2 away.

   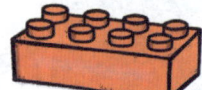 

Colour the number of bricks that she has left over.

 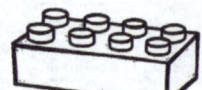 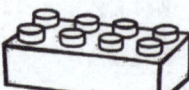  

Count the marbles. Then take 1 away.

3 take away 1 is

Count the skittles. Then take 3 away.

5 take away 3 is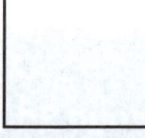

Count the bears.

Some bears fall off the train.

How many bears are still on the train?

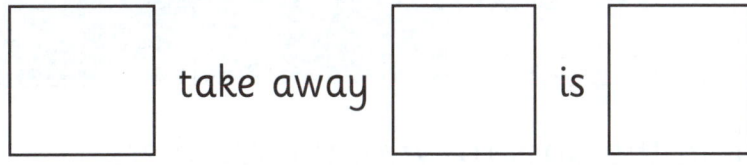

☐ take away ☐ is ☐

Draw the right card to fill in the space.

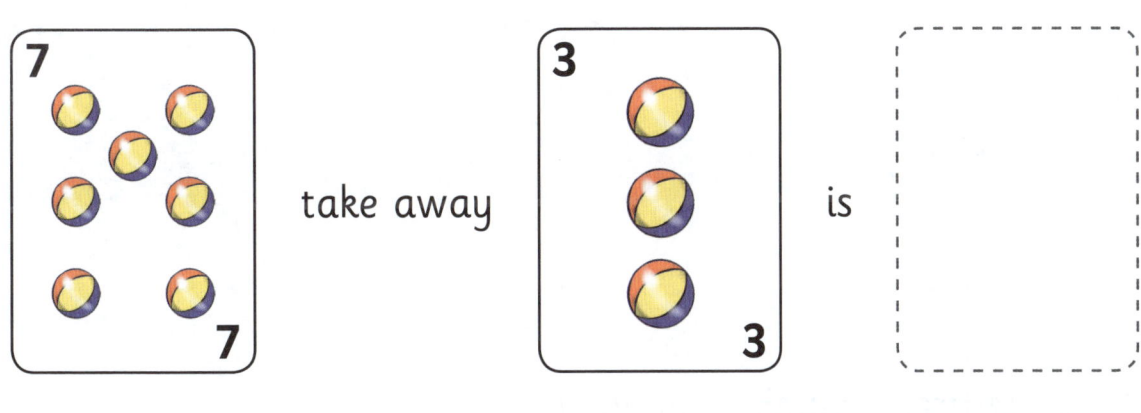

Keep up the good work! Tick the box.

The Numbers 11-20

How It Works

These numbers come after 10.

11 12 13 14 15 16 17 18 19 20

Count the candles.

There are **15** candles.

Now Try These

Join the dots to write the numbers.
Then say the numbers out loud.

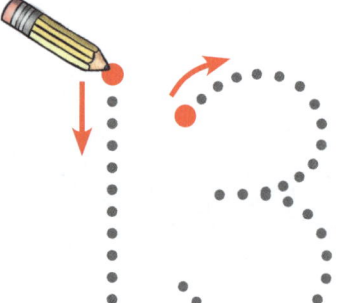 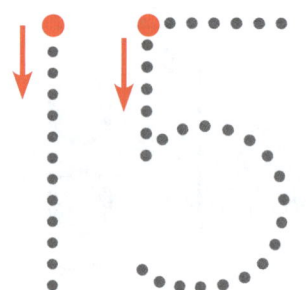 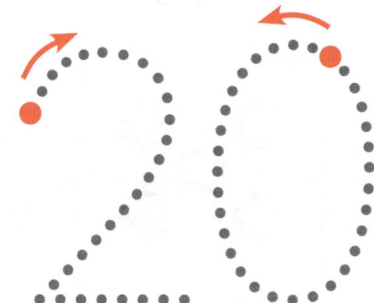

Circle gingerbread number nineteen.

How many biscuits has Martin made?

biscuits

Count the sandwiches in each set. Circle the set that has 13.

Sasha has made some pizzas.

How many of these toppings has she used altogether?

 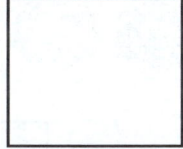   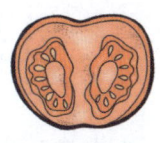     

You're really cooking now! Tick the box.

More Adding

How It Works

Count forwards to add. 6 + 3 = ?

6 7 8 9

So 6 + 3 = 9.

The + sign means add. The = sign means equals.

Now Try These

Add up the carrots. Draw the answer.

 +  =

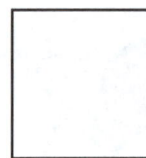 + 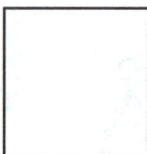 =

Count forwards to add up the cauliflowers.

 +  =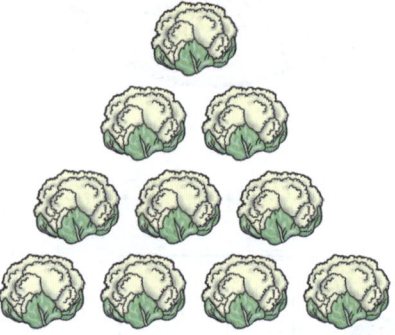

7 8 9 10

 7 + 3 =

Add each pair of numbers. Write the total in the box.

Match pairs of plates that add up to 10 beans (🫘).

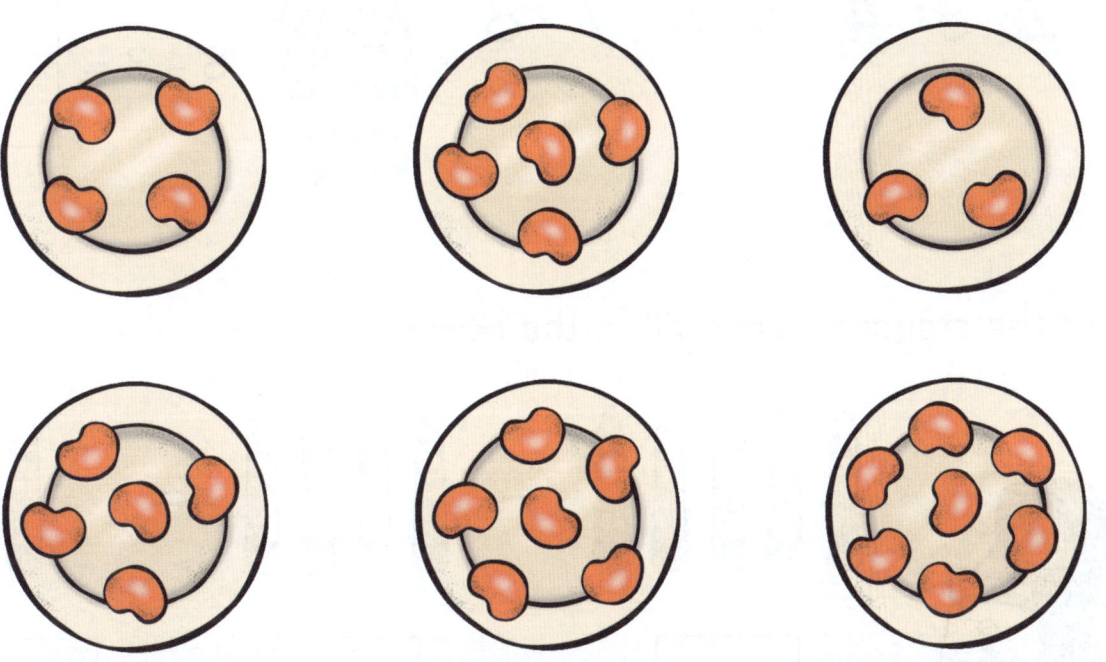

I knew I could count on you! Tick the box.

11

More Taking Away

How It Works

Count backwards to take away. 6 – 4 = ?

2   3   4   5   6

So 6 – 4 = 2.

The – sign means take away.

Now Try These

Count 8 paint pots. Then take 3 away.

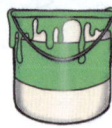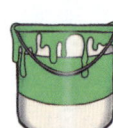

How many pots are left?

1 2 3 4 5 6 7 8

8 – 3 = ☐

Count the crayons. Then fill in the boxes.

  –  =

☐ – ☐ = ☐

Dean has 7 paint brushes. He gives 4 away.
How many paint brushes does he have left? Circle the number.

What is 9 – 6? Colour all the shapes with the answer.

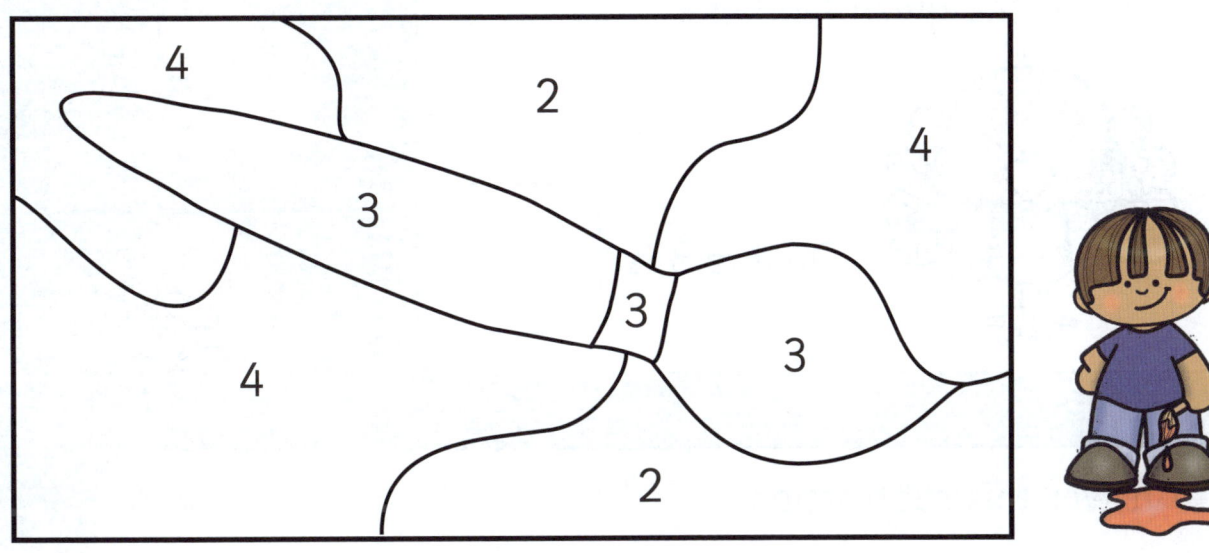

Write the answer to the subtraction below.
Circle the dice with that many dots.

You're doing great! Pop a tick in the box.

Turkey Trouble

Solve the puzzles to find your way through the maze.

1 Add up the caterpillars.

 + 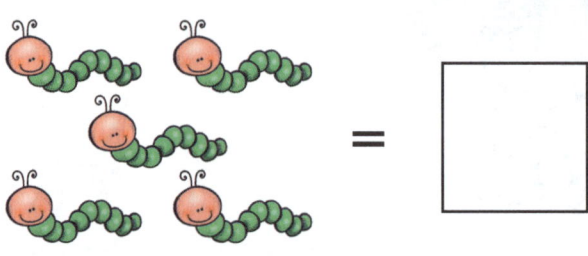 = ☐

2 Look at the green feathers.

 Double 3 is ☐

3 Answer this subtraction.

  −  = ☐

4 Draw the next shape in the pattern.

  ☐

5 What number is missing from this list?

Draw a path to the centre of the maze. You must pass over the answers to the puzzles in the correct order. Avoid any wrong answers and all the hedgehogs!

Odd and Even Numbers

How It Works

Count in twos to find odd and even numbers.

Odd numbers start at **1**:

1 2 3 4 5 6 7 8 9

Odd numbers of things can't be put in pairs — they have an odd one out.

Even numbers start at **2**:

1 2 3 4 5 6 7 8 9

Even numbers of things can be put in pairs.

Now Try These

How many turnips () are in the pot?
Is this number odd or even? Circle the right word.

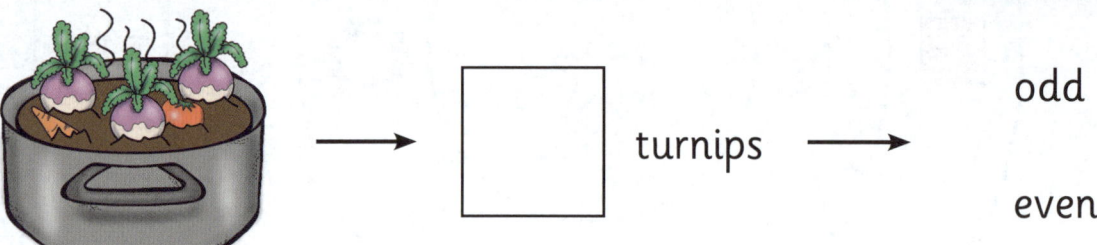

odd

even

Colour all the dice showing even numbers.

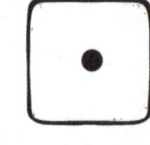

Tick the odd number of logs.

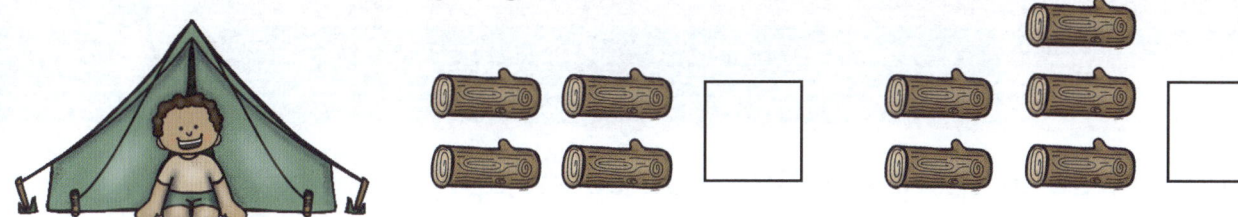

How many fingers are held up?
Is this number odd or even? Circle the right word.

odd

even

Look at this picture:

Count each thing in the picture.
Is the number odd or even? Tick the right box.

	odd	even		odd	even
chair	☐	☐	tree	☐	☐
tent	☐	☐	ant	☐	☐

You're even better than I thought! Tick that box.

Ordering

How It Works

Numbers go in the order that you count up.
Put 7, 5, 6 in order:

7 5 6

1 2 3 4 5 6 7 8 9

The order is 5, 6, 7.

Now Try These

Join the dots in order.
What do you see?

5
   6   7
4
3   8

2
      9
1

Colour the balloon with the correct number.

 **6** is **greater** than  8  7  5  9

 **18** is **less** than  16  14  17  20

Put the parade in the right order.

What does the parade look like when it's in order?

The balloons are flying in order. Write in the missing numbers.

Write the numbers in order.

You've got everything in order, so tick the box!

Doubling

How It Works

Doubling means having **2 lots** of the same number.

So double 3 is **6**.

Now Try These

Count the camels to fill in the boxes.

Double  is

Double ☐ is ☐

Count the meerkats in the desert.
Tick the set with double this number.

Double 2 is ☐

Colour in four more pots.

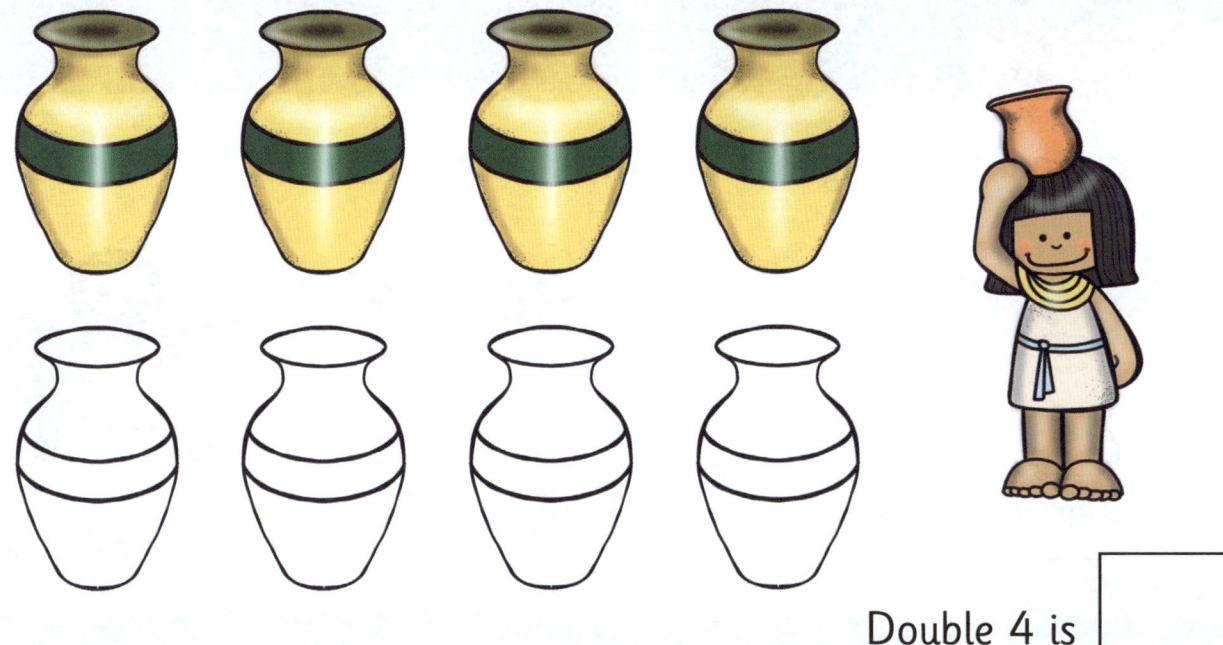

Double 4 is

Circle the crocodiles whose top teeth and bottom teeth make a double.

Draw 5 more teeth to make a double.

Double 5 is

You're doing well! Tick the box.

Halving

How It Works

Halving means sharing into **2 equal parts**.

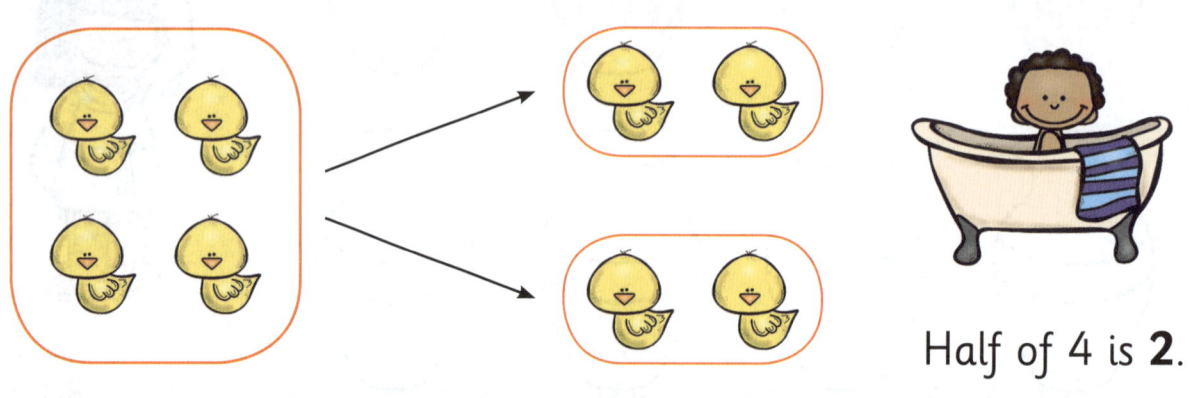

Half of 4 is **2**.

Now Try These

Share the toothbrushes into 2 equal groups. Circle each group.

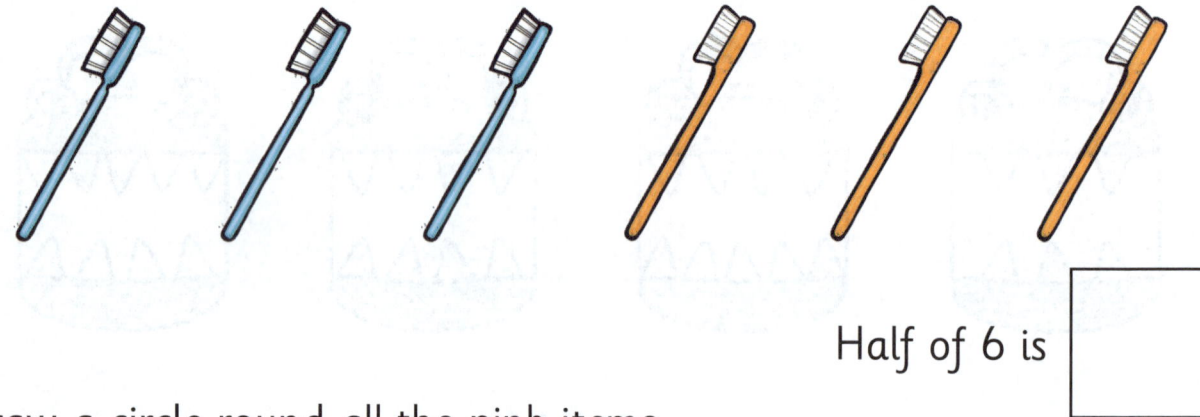

Half of 6 is ☐

Draw a circle round all the pink items.

Half of 8 is ☐

Tick the items that are shared equally.

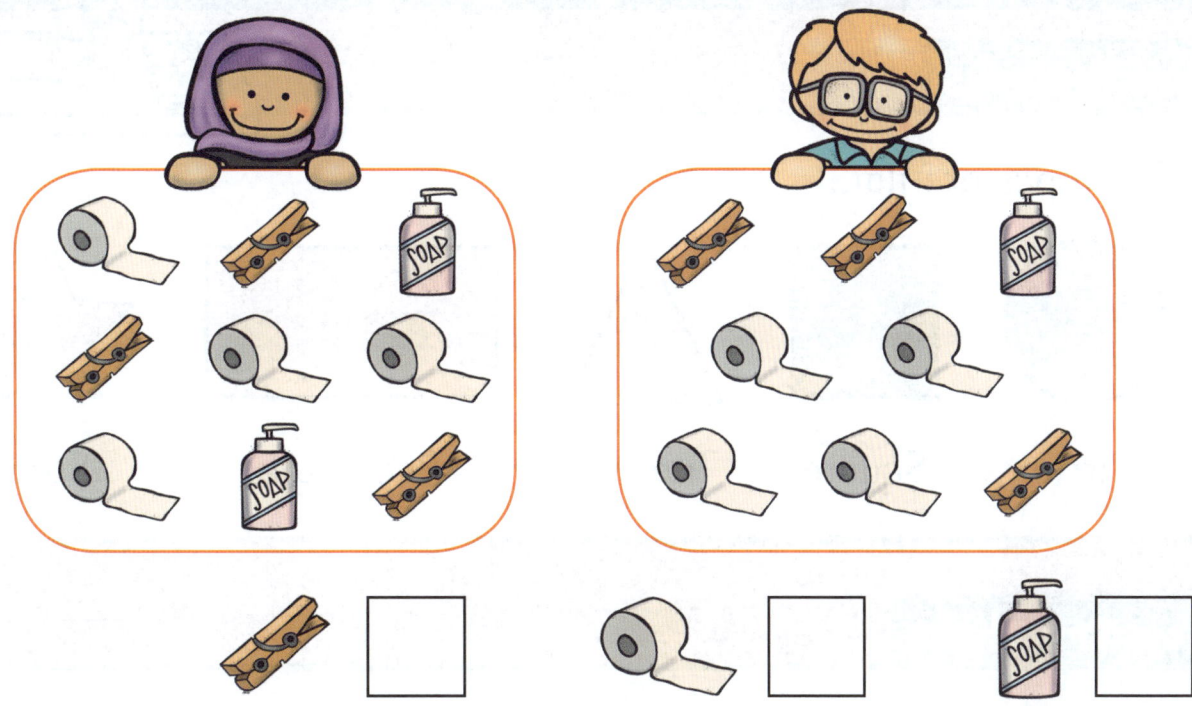

Colour the white towels to share them equally.

6 shared between 2 is ☐

Tick in the box — you've earned it!

2D Shapes

How It Works

2D shapes are flat.

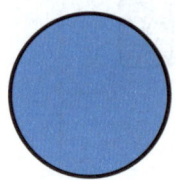    

Circle   Square   Triangle   Rectangle   Star

Now Try These

Join up the stars. What shape have you made?

Colour the squares blue and the rectangles green.

  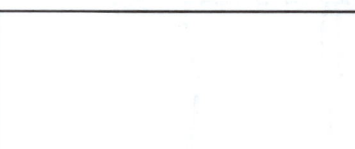

Match the words to the objects.

circle   square   triangle   rectangle   star

How many circles can you find below?

circles

Fantastic! You're all done, so tick the box.

3D Shapes

How It Works

These are 3D shapes. These shapes are solid — they're not flat.

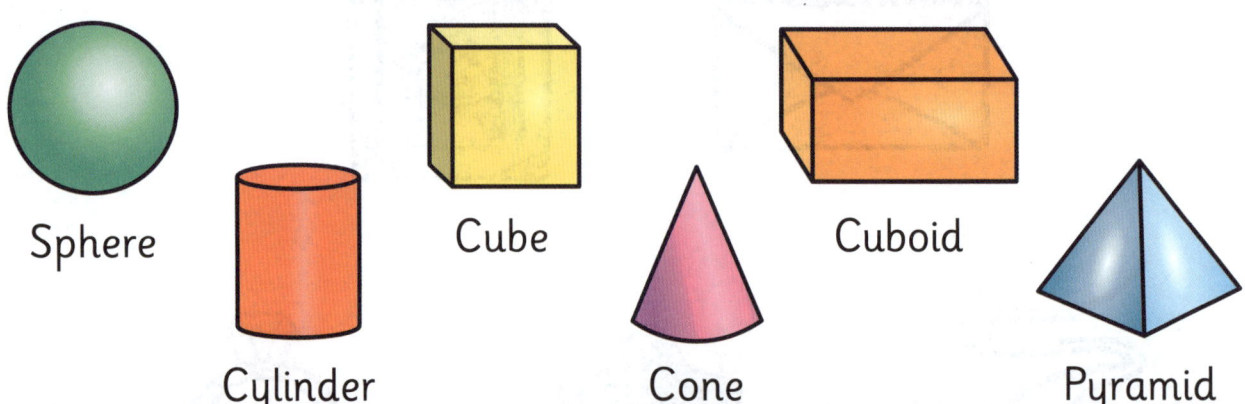

Now Try These

Count the cubes in each tower.

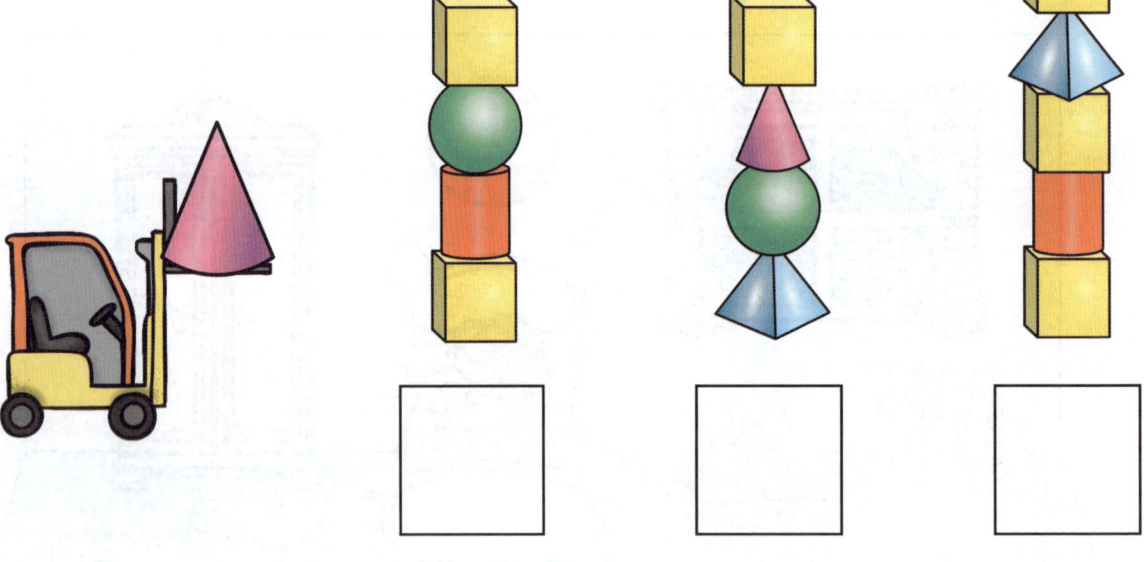

Circle the spheres.

Match each word with two objects.

cone

cylinder **pyramid**

Circle the cubes and cuboids below.

You know these shapes well. Tick the box!

Patterns

How It Works

A pattern repeats over and over.

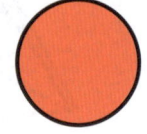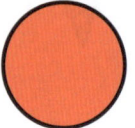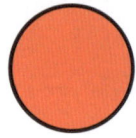

The next shape is

Now Try These

Draw the next shape in each pattern.

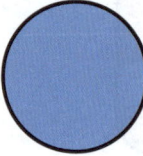

- -

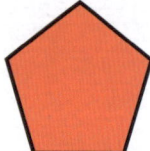

Colour the shapes to match each pattern.

- -

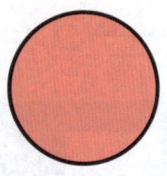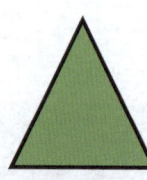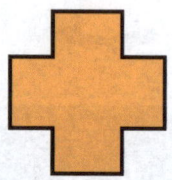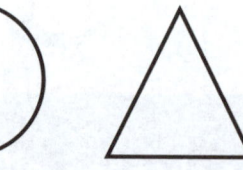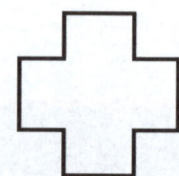

Who is missing from each pattern?

    ?

  ?

Draw a line to continue the pattern.
Go round any shape that doesn't match the pattern.

Great work! Award yourself a tick in the box.

Colour by Numbers

Colour in the shapes. Which toy do you see?

1 ■ (black) 2 ■ (orange) 3 ■ (pink) 4 ■ (grey) 5 ■ (light green) 6 ■ (light blue) 7 ■ (yellow)

8 ■ (brown) 9 ■ (light grey) 10 ■ (pink/magenta) 11 ■ (purple) 12 ■ (blue) 13 ■ (green)

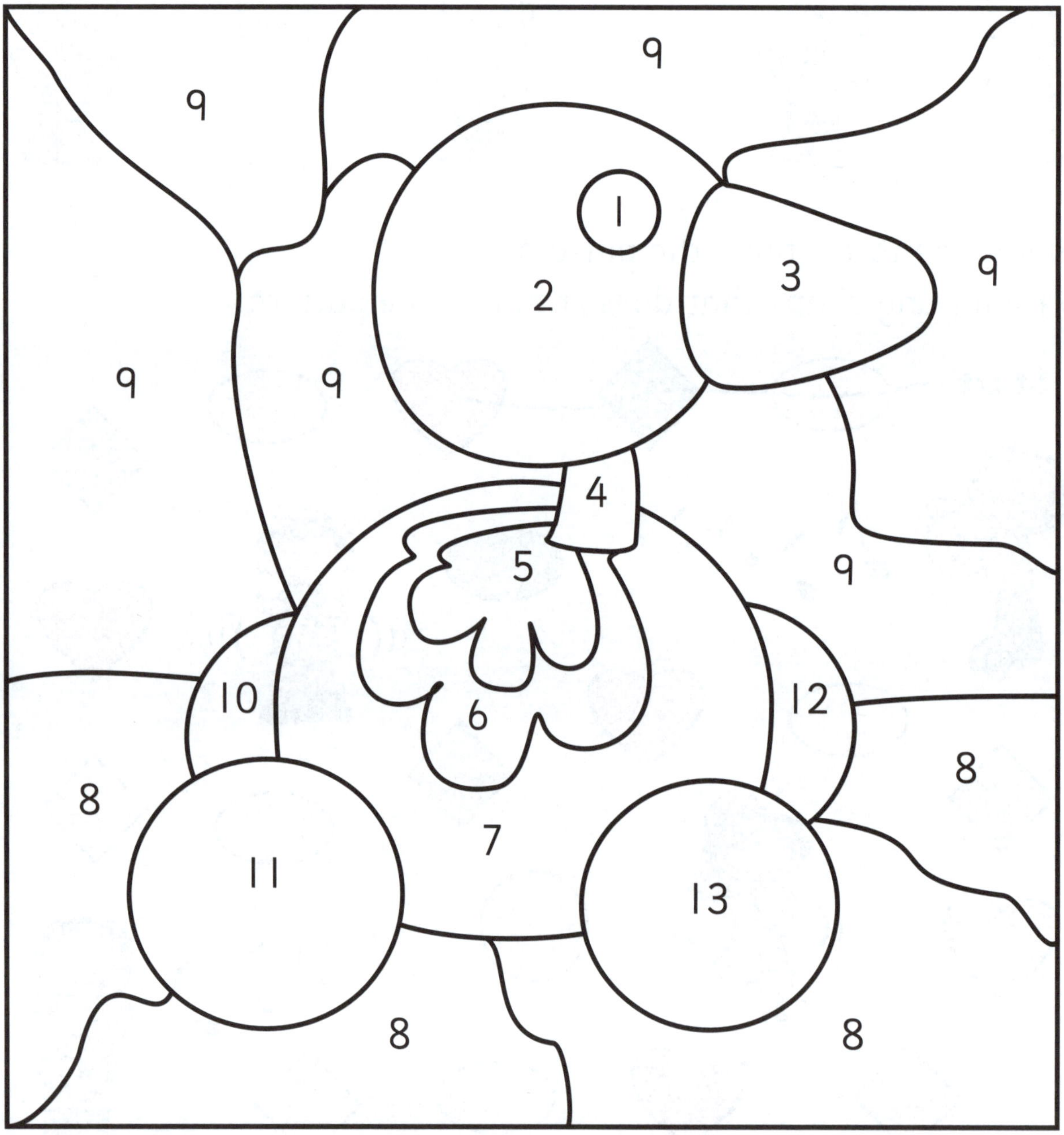